FRÉDÉRIC CHOPIN

Fantasy in F Minor, Barcarolle, Berceuse and Other Works for Solo Piano

Edited by Carl Mikuli

DOVER PUBLICATIONS, INC.

NEW YORK

Published in Canada by General Publishing Company, Ltd., 30 Lesmill Road, Don Mills, Toronto, Ontario.
Published in the United Kingdom by Constable and Company, Ltd.

This Dover edition, first published in 1989, is a republication of Vol. 14 *(Verschiedene Werke)* and portions of Vols. 5 *(Polonaisen)*, 9 *(Rondos)*, 12 *(Variationen)*, and 13 *(Fantasien)* of *Fr. Chopin's Pianoforte-Werke revidirt und mit Fingersatz versehen (zum grössten Theil nach des Autors Notirungen) von Carl Mikuli,* originally published by Fr. Kistner, Leipzig, n.d. (Foreword dated 1879). The editor's Foreword in the original German has been replaced by an English translation.

Manufactured in the United States of America
Dover Publications, Inc., 31 East 2nd Street, Mineola, N.Y. 11501

Library of Congress Cataloging-in-Publication Data

Chopin, Frédéric, 1810–1849.
    [Piano music. Selections]
    Fantasy in F minor, Barcarolle, Berceuse, and other works for solo piano.

    Reprint. Originally published: Leipzig: F. Kistner, 1879? Originally published in series: Fr. Chopin's Pianoforte-Werke. With new English translation of the foreword.
    Contents: Fantasy in F minor, op. 49 (1841)—Barcarolle, op. 60 (1845–46)—Berceuse, op. 57 (1843–44)—[etc.]
    1. Piano music. I. Mikuli, Carl. II. Title.
M22.C545M325 1989   88-754531
ISBN 0-486-25950-1

Foreword

INVITED BY THE music publisher Fr. Kistner of Leipzig to undertake the preparation of a complete edition of the works of my unforgettable teacher Frédéric Chopin, it was only with difficulty that I was able to arrive at a mutually agreeable response, in view of the great challenges of this highly responsible task. Whatever the inevitable misgivings, however, they could not override the reverence felt for the immortal master. This reverence had for some time urgently demanded that the veto of tradition be raised in opposition to the recklessly capricious textual alterations freely indulged in since his death, and that the composer's ideas and wishes be finally given the weight they deserve, clearly and without falsification.

As regards the existing editions of Chopin's works, the situation is as follows: Even the oldest French, German, and English original editions—let alone the later disfigured reprints—differ from one another in many passages, sometimes even in the number of bars within individual sections. Now, the available Parisian original editions have the advantage that during their engraving they could be, and in fact were, given to the composer for proofreading more often than the foreign German and English editions; while, on the other hand, these last, since they were for the most part engraved later than the French editions, contain here and there subsequent changes or improvements by Chopin himself. My friend and fellow pupil Thomas Telefsen, who had the fortune to be in uninterrupted contact with Chopin up until the composer's last breath, was in a perfect position to provide faithful versions for the edition begun by Richault. Unfortunately, a persistent disease leading to Telefsen's death interrupted this work, with the result that innumerable engraving errors remain uncorrected in the music.

The composer's autographs—a large number of which I have had the opportunity to study, since Telefsen and I copied many of them for him—are rife with careless errors and obvious slips of the pen (although the music is carefully worked out). They contain numerous wrong notes, note values, transpositions and clefs, omissions of chord members and dots, and mistakes in the extent of *8va* indications and in phrasing marks. An appeal to these original manuscripts as if to an irrefutable argument—however natural such an appeal might seem— proves in these circumstances to be the very opposite of incontestable; in fact such authority must be recognized as virtually illusory. The editor of a new edition who is dependent on such unreliable sources is thus only too easily induced to follow his own more-or-less legitimate judgment (which is in any event influenced by his own definite taste) in choosing from the many versions one that seems to him appropriate and probable—when not actually taking it on himself to *improve on* poor Chopin!

In view of such conditions, one would have to doubt the possibility of a correct Chopin edition if other means could not be employed. Luckily, however, they exist, and since I happened to be in a position to use these hitherto completely ignored but in fact essential sources, I could only regard it as a sacred trust to undertake the labor of a purified edition of Chopin's works.

To begin with, I myself possess volumes, mainly from the Paris edition, in which Chopin at my lessons corrected errors with his own hand as they came to light over time; still other volumes in which I noted down his comments during other students' lessons, which Chopin permitted me to attend as a special favor; and, finally, several more volumes with abundant corrections in his own hand, which the late Countess Delfina Potocka, Chopin's friend and student of many years, presented to me during her residence in Lemberg [Lvov].

Along with the inevitable discovery in this valuable material of the certain answer to many questions, the quite exceptional cooperation of highly distinguished students and friends of the master, who most generously assisted me in word and deed, gave rise to my well-founded hopes that, guided by a still-living tradition and grounded in the composer's own corrections, this edition would succeed in restoring the authentic text and in making further mutilation forever impossible.

Above all, I must mention here, with heartfelt thanks, Marceline the Princess Czartoryska of Krakow and Friederike Streicher, née Müller, of Vienna (the dedicatee of op. 46), who, during several years of study and on many other occasions, had numerous opportunities to hear their teacher perform his own works, so that their reminiscences were of the greatest significance to the editor. Not only through correspondence but also for weeks in person, we conscientiously perused the music from note to note, referring to numerous corrections and notations in the composer's hand, which they kept like a holy relic in their copies of the music.

I feel no less obliged to thank Camille Dubois, née Omeara, of Paris, and Vera Rubio, née von Kologriwof, of Florence, both superb pianists whose considerable talent had enjoyed the particular attention of the master; and finally Dr. Ferdinand von Hiller, director of the Rheinische Musikschule in Cologne, and Auguste Franchomme, professor at the Paris Conservatory, faithful and beloved friends of the deceased composer. They were all most generous in giving crucial information regarding corrections in many passages, and Mr. Franchomme particularly for the chamber music, on which he was in part a collaborator.

I must note here that the fingering of this edition comes in large part from Chopin himself; where it does not, it is at least worked out in accordance with his principles, so as, in the editor's opinion, to simplify the execution of the composer's wishes.

On the great significance of Chopin the composer, an almost unanimous judgment has long since been reached. The enthusiastic cry of Robert Schumann (in an 1831 review of Chopin's op. 2, *Là ci darem la mano*, in his *Allgemeine Musikzeitung*), "Hut ab, ihr Herrn! Ein Genie!" ["Hats off, gentlemen! A genius!"], proved to be a truly prophetic cry, as well, in view of the uninterrupted succession of masterpieces that followed, works that take a just place alongside the highest achievements in music by virtue of their novelty of melodic invention, nobility of expression, and harmony that is refined and always euphonious —never pretentious or affected despite its boldness—and by virtue of their introduction of a pioneering treatment of the instrument, and, above all, the enchantment of their ideal beauty. The two concertos (the earlier, in F minor, dedicated to Countess Delfina Potocka, was particularly dear to him); the Etudes, which founded a new school of pianism; the two great sonatas; the highly poetic and atmospheric Preludes and Nocturnes; the Scherzos, Ballades, and Impromptus—all carry the stamp of genius. If the Mazurkas and Polonaises, with their national hues inspired by faithful memory of the beloved fatherland and by lifelong, unrelieved, passionate longing for it, have a great and unsurpassed charm for Polish hearts, they have also garnered the warmest appreciation in the whole musical world. Their value bears absolutely no relation to the narrow frame into which they are compressed. They are brilliantly executed genre paintings in whose every bar the whole of Polish life pulses with accents at one moment noble, at the next rapturous or boisterously merry. Proud of its possession, his fatherland celebrates and loves him and will always count him among its greatest sons.

While Chopin the composer is now respected and honored by all true friends of art and connoisseurs, Chopin the pianist has remained almost unknown; what is worse, an entirely false impression of him in this respect has been generally circulated. According to that version, his playing was more that of a dreamer than that of a waking man—playing that was barely audible, consisting as it did of nothing but pianissimos and una cordas, highly uncertain or at least unclear because of poorly developed technique, and distorted into something totally arrhythmic by a constant rubato! This prejudice could not help being very detrimental to the rendering of his works even at the hands of highly capable artists who only desired to be utterly faithful. Incidentally, it is easy to explain.

Chopin played in public seldom and only unwillingly; "showing off" was alien to his nature. A sickliness of many years and a nervously overwrought temperament did not always allow him, in the concert hall, the composure necessary to exhibit unhindered the whole wealth of his resources. In select circles he rarely played anything but his smaller creations, and now and again excerpts from the larger ones. Thus it is not surprising that Chopin the pianist failed to achieve any wide recognition.

And yet Chopin possessed a highly developed technique, in complete command of the instrument. In all types of touch, the evenness of his scales and passagework was unsurpassed, indeed fabulous; under his hands the piano had no need to envy either the violin its bow or the wind instruments their living breath. The tones blended miraculously as in the loveliest song.

A true pianist's hand, not so much large as extremely supple, enabled him to arpeggiate the most widely disposed harmonies and to perform sweeping passagework, which he had introduced into the idiom of the piano as something never before dared, and all without the slightest exertion being evident, just as overall an agreeable freedom and ease particularly characterized his playing. At the same time, the tone that he could draw from the instrument was always huge, especially in the cantabiles; only Field could compare with him in this respect.

A virile, noble energy—energy without rawness—lent an overwhelming effect to the appropriate passages, just as elsewhere he could enrapture the listener through the tenderness—tenderness without affectation—of his soulful renditions. With all his intense personal warmth, his playing was nevertheless always moderate, chaste, refined, and occasionally even austerely reserved.

Unfortunately, in the trend of modern pianism, these fine distinctions, like so many others belonging to an ideal art movement, are thrown into the attic of "superseded ideas" that hinder progress, and a naked display of strength, not considering the capacity of the instrument, not even striving for the beauty of the sound to be shaped, today passes for large tone and energetic expression!

In keeping tempo Chopin was inflexible, and it will surprise many to learn that the metronome never left his piano. Even in his much-slandered rubato, one hand, the accompanying hand, always played in strict tempo, while the other—singing, either indecisively hesitating or entering ahead of the beat and moving more quickly with a certain impatient vehemence, as in passionate speech—freed the truth of the musical expression from all rhythmic bonds.

Although Chopin for the most part played his own compositions, his memory—as rich as it was accurate—mastered all the great and beautiful works of keyboard literature—above all Bach, though it is hard to say whether he loved Bach or Mozart more. His execution of this music was unequaled. With the little G major trio by Mozart (played with Alard and Franchomme) he literally bewitched the blasé Parisian public in one of his last concerts. Naturally Beethoven was just as close to his heart. He had a great predilection for C. M. von Weber's works, particularly the Konzertstück and the E minor and Ab major sonatas; for Hummel's Fantasy, Septet, and concertos; and for Field's Ab major concerto and Nocturnes, for which he improvised the most captivating ornaments. Of the virtuoso music of every degree of quality—which in his time terribly crowded out everything else—I never saw one piece on his piano stand, and I doubt if anyone else ever did. He very rarely took the opportunity to hear such works in the concert hall, though such opportunities were frequently presented and even urged on him, but in contrast he was an enthusiastic regular at Habeneck's Société de Concerts and Alard and Franchomme's string-quartet performances.

It should be of interest to many readers to learn something of Chopin the teacher, if only in general outline.

Teaching was something he could not easily avoid, in his capacity as an artist and with his social attachments in Paris; but far from regarding it as a heavy burden, Chopin dedicated all his strength to it for several hours a day with genuine pleasure. Admittedly he placed great demands on the talent and industry of the student. There were often "leçons orageuses," as they were called in school parlance, and many a lovely eye left the high altar of the Cité d'Orléans, rue St Lazare, in tears, yet without bearing the least resentment against the greatly beloved master. For it was this rigor so hard to satisfy, the feverish intensity with which the master strove to raise his disciples to his own pinnacle, the refusal to cease in the repetition of a passage until it was understood, that constituted a guarantee that he had the pupil's progress at heart. A holy artistic zeal glowed through him; every word from his lips was stimulating and inspiring. Often individual lessons lasted literally for several hours, until the exhaustion of master and pupil won out.

At the beginning of study, Chopin generally sought to free the student's hand from all stiffness and any convulsive, spasmodic movement, and thus to produce in him the first condition of beautiful playing—"souplesse," and along with it the independence of the fingers. Untiringly he taught that the appropriate exercises should not be merely mechanical but rather should enlist the whole will of the student; therefore he would never require a mindless twenty- or forty-fold repetition (still today the extolled arcanum at so many schools), let alone a drill during which one could, according to Kalkbrenner's advice, simultaneously occupy oneself with reading(!). He dealt very thoroughly with the various types of touch, especially full-toned legato.

As gymnastic aids, he recommended the bending in and out of the wrist, the repeated wrist attack, the stretching of the fingers—always with a serious warning against fatigue. He insisted that scales be played with large tone, as legato as possible, first very slowly and only gradually increasing the tempo, with metronomic evenness. Bending the hand inward would, he claimed, facilitate turning the thumb under and crossing the other fingers over it. The scales with many black keys (B major, F# major, Db major) were the first to be studied, the last—as the most difficult—being C major. In a similar sequence, he first assigned Clementi's Preludes and Exercises, a work that he valued very highly for its usefulness. According to Chopin, the evenness of scales (and also arpeggios) was founded not only on the greatest possible equality in finger strength and a thumb completely unimpeded in crossing under and over—to be achieved by five-finger exercises—but far more on a sideways movement of the hand, not jerky but always evenly gliding, with the elbow hanging down completely and freely; this he sought to illustrate on the keyboard by a glissando. As studies he assigned a selection from Cramer's Etudes, Clementi's *Gradus ad Parnassum*, the *Finishing Studies in Style* by Moscheles (which he was very fond of), Bach's suites, and individual fugues from the *Well-Tempered Clavier*.

To an extent, he also numbered Field's and his own Nocturnes among these piano studies, since in them the student could learn to recognize, love, and execute beautifully flowing singing tone and legato, partly through a grasp of his explanations, partly through intuitive perception and imitation (he played these works constantly for his students). In double notes and chords he demanded precisely simultaneous attacks; breaking the chord was permitted only where the composer himself specified it. In trills, which he generally stipulated should begin on the upper auxiliary, he insisted less on rapidity than on absolute evenness, and the trill endings had to be calm and unrushed.

For the turn (gruppetto) and the appoggiatura, he recommended the great Italian singers as models. He required that octaves be played with the wrist, but cautioned that they must not lose any fullness of tone as a result. Only to significantly advanced students did he assign his Etudes, op. 10 and op. 25.

Concertos and sonatas by Clementi, Mozart, Bach, Handel, Scarlatti, Dussek, Field, Hummel, Ries, and Beethoven; then, works by Weber, Moscheles, Mendelssohn, Hiller, and Schumann and his own works were the pieces that appeared on the music stand, in a sequence carefully ordered by difficulty. Above all, it was correct phrasing to which Chopin devoted the greatest attention. On the subject of bad phrasing, he often repeated the apt observation that it seemed to him as if someone were reciting a speech in a language he didn't know, a speech laboriously memorized by rote, in which the reciter not only did not observe the natural length of the syllables but would even make stops in the middle of individual words. The pseudo musician who phrased badly revealed in a similar way that music was not his native language but rather something strange and incomprehensible, and must, like the reciter, fail to produce any effect on the listener through his performance. In the notation of fingering, particularly the most personally characteristic fingering, Chopin was not sparing. Pianists owe him thanks for his great innovations in fingering, which because of their effectiveness soon became established, though authorities such as Kalkbrenner were initially truly horrified by them. Chopin unhesitatingly employed the thumb on the black keys; he crossed it even under the fifth finger (admittedly with a decided bending-in of the wrist) when this could facilitate the performance or lend it more serenity and evenness. He often took two successive notes with one and the same finger (and not only in the transition from a black key to a white one), without the slightest break in the tonal flow becoming noticeable. He frequently crossed the longer fingers over each other, without the help of the thumb (see Etude no. 2 from op. 10), and not only in passages where it was made absolutely necessary by the thumb's holding a key. The fingering of chromatic thirds based on this principle (as he indicates it in Etude no. 5 from op. 25) offers, to a much greater degree than the then-usual method, the possibility of the most beautiful legato in the fastest tempo with an altogether calm hand. As for shading, he adhered strictly to a genuinely gradual crescendo and decrescendo. On declamation and on performance in general, he gave his pupils invaluable and meaningful advice and hints, but certainly exerted a far stronger influence by repeatedly playing for his students not only individual passages but entire works, and with a conscientiousness and enthusiasm that he rarely displayed in the concert hall. Often the entire lesson would pass without the student's having played more than a few measures, while Chopin, interrupting and correcting him on the Pleyel upright (the student always played on an outstanding concert piano, and was required to practice only on the finest instruments), offered the warm, living ideal of the highest beauty for his admiration and emulation. One could say without exaggeration that only his students knew Chopin the pianist in his full, quite unattainable greatness.

Chopin most insistently recommended ensemble playing, the cultivation of the best chamber music—but only in the company of highly accomplished musicians. Whoever could not find such opportunities was urged to seek a substitute in four-hand playing.

Just as insistently he advised his pupils to undertake thorough theoretical studies as early as possible, and most of them were grateful for his kind intercession when his friend Henri Reber (later professor at the Paris Conservatory), whom he respected highly both as a theorist and as a composer, agreed to instruct them. In every situation the great heart of the master was open to his students. A sympathetic and fatherly friend, he inspired them to incessant efforts, rejoiced genuinely in every new accomplishment, and always had an encouraging word for the wavering and fainthearted.

Lemberg, September 1879   CARL MIKULI

Contents

Fantasy in F Minor, Op. 49

8   Fantasy in F Minor

Barcarolle, Op. 60

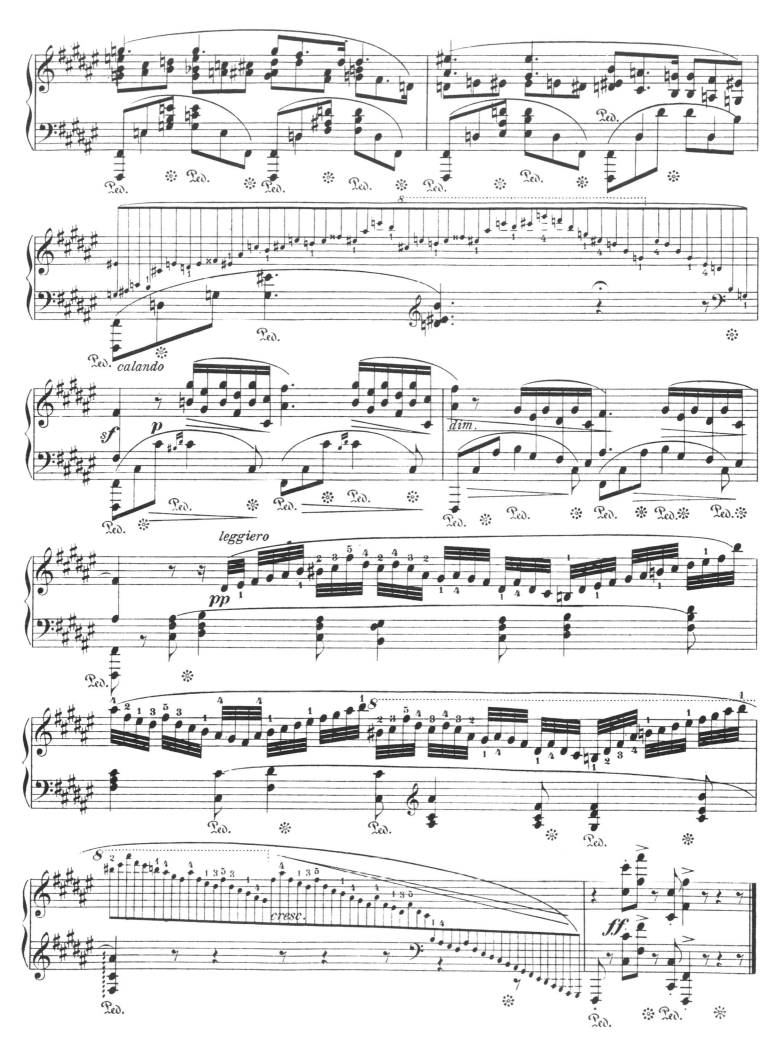

Berceuse, Op. 57

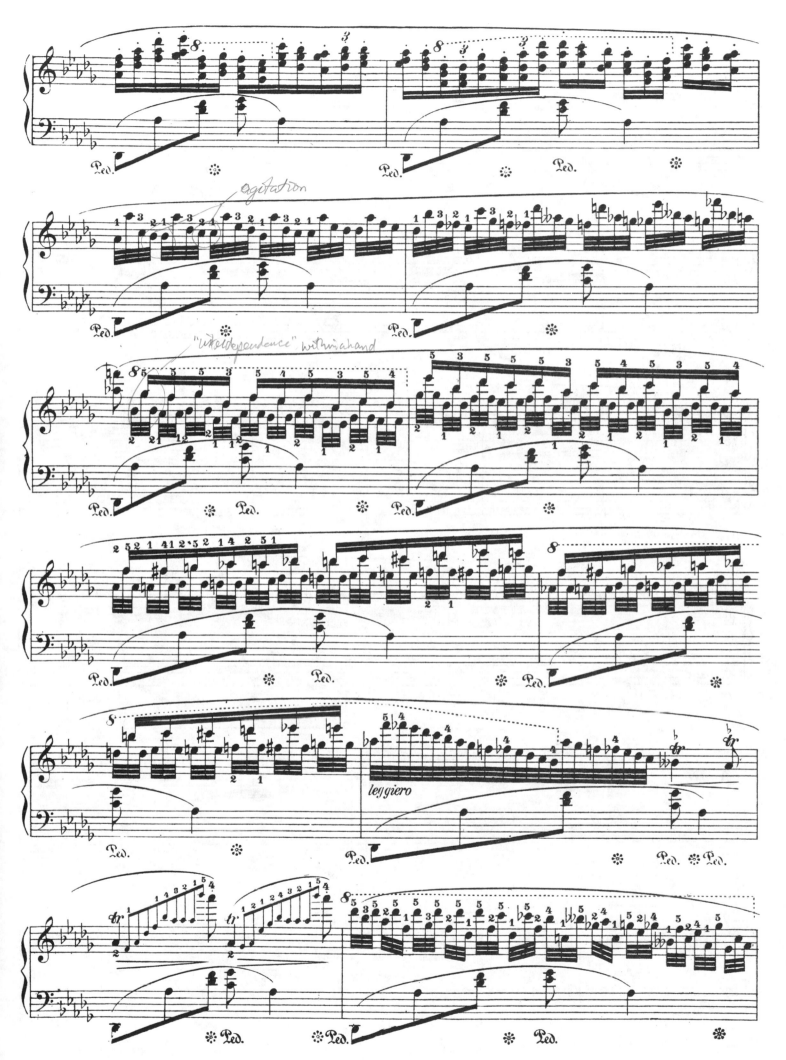

Bolero, Op. 19

Introduction.
Allegro molto.

Tarantelle, Op. 43

Allegro de Concert, Op. 46

Andante spianato
Introduction to the Grand Polonaise for piano and orchestra, Op. 22

Funeral March in C Minor, Op. 72, No. 2

TRIO.

Three Ecossaises, Op. 72, No. 3

Introduction and Variations on "Je vends des scapulaires" from Hérold's Ludovic

Introduction.
Allegro maestoso. ♩ = 118.

Variations on "Je vends des scapulaires"

Introduction and Variations on a German Air
("Der Schweizerbub")

THEMA.
Andantino. ($\dot{}$ = 54.)

p semplice senza ornamenti

VAR. III.
Tranquillamente. (♩ = 60.)

Variation No. 6 from the Hexameron

Rondo in C Minor, Op. 1

Rondo "à la Mazur," Op. 5

114 Rondo "à la Mazur"

Introduction and Rondo, Op. 16